The Pennsylvania Lion or Panther

(REVISED EDITION)

*"Une panthere ou un lion, me disait
je, serait loge a souhait la dedans!"*
— *Bombonnel*

Extinct
Pennsylvania
Animals

The Altoona Tribune Publishing Co.
ALTOONA, PENNA.
1 9 1 7

INDEX.

I. PREFACE.

THE object of this pamphlet is to produce a narrative blending the history and romance of the once plentiful Lion of Pennsylvania. While pages have been written in natural histories describing this animal's unpleasant characteristics, not a word has been said in its favor. It has never even had an apologetic. In reality the Pennsylvania Lion needs no defenders, as those who understand him realize the nobility of his nature. From reading John W. Godman's "American Natural History," published in 1828, one would imagine that the Pennsylvania Lion, or, as it is most commonly called, the panther, was a most terrible beast. Among other things he says: "In the daytime the cougar is seldom seen, but its peculiar cry frequently thrills the experienced traveler with horror, while camping in the forest for the night." Even Mary Jemison, "The White Woman of the Genessee," speaks of "the terrifying shrieks of the ferocious panther," as she heard it in her childhood days on Marsh Creek, Franklin County. In reality the panther was an inoffensive creature, desiring only to be let alone, yet brave when attacked by dogs, and respectful of man. A single hunter in St. Lawrence County, New York, met five panthers together, of which, with his dog and gun, he killed three at the time and the next day the other two. The first settlers finding it in the woods set out to kill it as they did

5

with every other living thing from the paroquet to the heath-cock, from the northern hare to the pine marten, from the passenger pigeon to the wild turkey, without trying to study it, or give it a chance. Economically the panther was of great value for the hide, meat, and oil, and as the finest game animal which Pennsylvania produced. As former Governor Glynn, of New York, said in a message to the Legislature, "Game should be conserved to furnish a cheap food supply." In the following pages will be found the bulk of the information which the writer has been able to collect on the subject of the panther in Pennsylvania. It has been prepared from the point of view of the old hunters, whom the writer has interviewed. While there are some statements which are liable to be declared scientifically incorrect, they are printed for what they are worth, as the authorities were as reliable as *unscientific* observers can be. The writer has consulted practically every book which contains a mention of the panther in the Keystone State, and also many other works on the cougar of the United States and Central and South America. He does not seek to "split hairs" and make the Pennsylvania Lion a separate variety, greater or grander than its relatives in other parts. The statement is herein made that Pennsylvania panthers were the largest known in the East, and this the writer believes to be correct. The romantic part of the panther's sojourn among us has been dilated upon whenever possible. This animal, above all others, added most to the legendary lore of the State. But the chief effort of these pages will be to disprove many of the stories derogatory to the animal, to give a hearing to its side of the case and a wider knowledge of its beauty and usefulness. This is done in case a time should come when "red-blooded" sportsmen will decide to reintroduce the panther as our leading game animal. Then there would be at least one published work which would show the misjudged "cougar" in a favorable light. Though perhaps lacking in scientific exactness, these pages would contain a brief for its existence. Southern panthers may still visit the wilder localities of Pennsylvania, and a wider knowledge of the animal might help prevent a general onslaught against these wanderers. In this connection it might be well to state that the wandering panthers are smaller than those which held their fixed abode in a single valley. In Algeria, where wandering leopards or "panthers" are found, they are called Berrani, whereas those which remain in one locality are called Dolly. The Berrani, (the Hunting Leopard) strangely enough, is smaller than the Dolly. Natural history has many parallels, coincidences and mysteries. All of them teach us the wonders of existence and should make us deal gently with every form of God's lesser creatures. We have no right to say which animals shall be destroyed and which spared. Just as we look with scorn on the wasteful methods of the old-time lumbermen of Pennsylvania, we will before long cherish the same opinion of the men who wantonly destroyed the wild life of the Commonwealth.

II. HISTORY.

THE history of the panther seems to be as old as
the Indians themselves. The Erie tribe who
were blotted out by the Iroquois in 1656 were
called the Yenresh, or "the long tailed," which was
Gallicised into "Eri," hence Erie, "the place of the
panther." The French called the Erie, "Nation du
Chat," or Cat Nation, which was simply a translation
of Yenresh, the name of the panther. Nation du Chat
means "Panther Nation," which is the real name of
the Erie.

From the earliest times the Pennsylvania lion has
been unjustly feared. The first Swedish settlers on
the Delaware hunted it unmercifully. They could not
but believe that an animal which howled so hideously
at night must be a destroyer of human life. When
William Penn first landed at Philadelphia the range of
the panther still extended to the outskirts of the city
of Brotherly Love. In a letter to his friends in Eng-
land, written during his first visit to his province, he
said: "Of living creatures, fish, fowl, and the beasts
of the wood, here are divers sorts, some for food and
profit, and some for profit only; for food as well as
profit, the elk, as big as a small ox; deer, bigger than
ours, beaver, raccoon, rabbits, squirrels, and some eat
young bear and commend it. The creatures for profit
only, by skin or fur, and which are natural to these
parts, are the wild cat, panther, otter, wolf, fisher,

9

minx, muskrat, etc." This shows that the sagacious
Quaker was awake to the commercial possibilities of
the panther and other animals. On a number of occa-
sions he expresses himself in favor of the protection
of fur-bearing animals, except when their coats were
in prime condition. Certain of the Mingo Indians
hated the panther, classing it with the wolf and wild
cat, as one of the few animals which were at perpetual
war with their God of the chase, Kanistagia. By the
beginning of the eighteenth century the panther was
driven back as far as the western limits of the present
Chester County. By 1750 it was rarely found East of
the Blue Mountains. Here it made its stand for more
than three-quarters of a century. By 1840 it was
driven further West, its limits being approximately a
line drawn across the State in a Northeasterly direction, beginning at the Eastern border of Fulton County, through Perry County, thence along the North
Branch to Wilkes-Barre, and from thence across to
Honesdale. By 1870 the range was closed in to the
following counties: Clearfield, Centre, Mifflin, Clinton, Potter, Lycoming and Susquehanna. By 1880
Clearfield, Centre and Mifflin contained the only native panthers, though wanderers from West Virginia
continued traveling through some of the Western and
Northern counties. In 1895 the range was limited to
two valleys only, viz: Havice and Treaster, in Mifflin
County, when the last native race of panthers disappeared. Dr. J. T. Rothrock, former Forestry Commissioner of Pennsylvania, heard the weird cry in Treas-

ter Valley, in 1893. Of all the animals of Pennsylvania the panther is by far the most picturesque, and has been treated in the most fantastic manner by early writers. In an old history of the Lenni-Lenape, published nearly a century ago, a writer states: "There are many animals which the Indians in Pennsylvania were accustomed to hunt, some on account of their value, and others because of the mischief they did. Among these the panther is a terrible animal. Its cry resembles that of a child, but this is interrupted by a peculiar bleating like that of a goat, which betrays it. It gnarls over its prey like a cat. It possesses astonishing strength and swiftness in leaping and seizing hogs, deer and other animals. When pursued, even with a small dog, it leaps into a tree, from which it darts upon its enemy. If the first shot misses, the hunter is in imminent danger. They do not, in common, attack men, but if hunters or travelers approach a covert, in which the panther has its young, their situation is perilous. Whoever flies from it is lost. It is, therefore, necessary for those threatened with an attack to withdraw gently, walking backward, and keeping their eyes fixed on the animal, and even if they miss an aim in shooting at it, to look at it steadfastly." It was these early inaccurate accounts which caused the public clamor against the Pennsylvania lion, resulting in the enactment of bounty laws and speedy extermination. In 1850, John Hamilton, a surveyor, encountered a female panther and two cubs crossing the Coudersport pike, going in the direction of Little

Chatham Run. Though within twenty feet of the huge female, the animal made no effort to molest the gentleman. So much for the great danger of approaching where "a panther has its young!" Dr. Caspar Wistar, Professor of Anatomy in the University of Pennsylvania, originally owned the land on which the towns of Loganton and Carroll, in Clinton County, now stand. As there were no railroads in those days, Dr. Wistar, when on his periodical visits to Sugar Valley, drove in his own conveyance, accompanied by Hercules, his faithful colored servant. Just previous to one of his visits, Henry Barner, a pioneer, whose "old homestead," near the mouth of Carroll Gap, is still standing, killed a panther in his front yard. He shot the monster, it is said, as it was about to spring at him. It was found to measure more than eleven feet from tip to tip. Upon reaching the neighborhood Dr. Wistar soon learned that an unusually large panther had been killed by Mr. Barner, and immediately proceeded to the home of the settler to ascertain the particulars of the capture. As he approached the dwelling he saw lying in the yard the grinning head of the panther in an advanced stage of decomposition, but, being prompted by a desire to further his scientific researches, he desired to procure it for dissection, regardless of its condition. Accordingly he ordered his servant to place the head in his carriage that he might take it to Philadelphia. This the Negro did, but for years afterward he would laugh about "dat limburger smell under de seat." This Negro's son became so impressed by the wonders of the forest life that he took employment as body-servant to Ario Pardee, the millionaire lumberman, and under the name of "Black Sam," was well known in the old-time lumber and hunting country in Central Pennsylvania.

III.   DESCRIPTION.

A FTER interviewing many old-time panther hunters and persons who saw the Pennsylvania lion
alive or recently killed, among them Jacob
Quiggle (1821-1911), John H. Chatham, George G.
Hastings, Seth Iredell Nelson (1809-1905), Clement
F. Herlacher and others, the writer has evolved the
following description of the Lion of Pennsylvania:
Body, long, slim, head large (averaging eight inches
in mature specimens, wide in proportion to length);
legs strong, short; forelegs like the African lion,
stouter than hind legs; tail, long and tufted at end;
color greyish about the eyes; hairs within the ears
grey, slightly tinged with yellow; exterior of ears
blackish; those portions of the lips which support the
whiskers, black; the remaining portion of the lip pale
chocolate; throat, grey; beneath the neck pale yellow.
General color, reddish in Potter County, shading from
a dull gray to a slate further South in the State. The
hide of a West Virginia pantheress killed on the
Greenbriar River, Pocohontas County, in 1901, three-
quarters grown, owned by Hon. C. K. Sober, of Lewisburg, has long white hair on chest and belly, a fluffy,
dark brown tail, culminating in a large tuft of black
hair, like the tip of the tail of an African lion. It
measured seven feet three inches from tip to tip.
Georges Buffon, whose French work on Natural His-

14

tory is an authority, in speaking of the *Cougar de Pennsylvanie,* says: "It is low on its legs, has a longer tail than the Western puma; it is described as five feet six inches in length, tail two feet six inches; height before, one foot nine inches; behind, one foot ten inches." Dr. C. Hart Merriam says that the head of the Adirondack panther was proportionately small. The head of the Pennsylvania panther, according to the concensus of opinion, was large and round. George G. Hastings says that the panthers he killed had heads "like bulldogs." Of the three mounted specimens now in existence, all of which are fortunately mounted with the skulls, the heads are large. The size of the head and jaws of the specimen in the Museum at State College, which is magnificently mounted, is the most noticeable feature of the manikin. The hair of the female panther was somewhat longer than the males. Many naturalists claim that the tails of the female cougars are shorter than the males. Pennsylvania panther hunters aver that the tails of the females were as long as the males, although very few females were captured. The Pennsylvania lion was known by a great variety of names. William Penn called it the panther—why, cannot be imagined; it is colored very differently from the *panthere* of Northern Africa, which he probably had in mind. The backwoodsmen called it the *painter;* there is a Painter Run in Tioga County, a Painterville in Westmoreland County, and painter hollows and painter rocks innumerable all over the State. Semi-humorous persons alluded to it as the

Pennsylvania lion, but this in turn has become its most dignified cognomen. It is interesting to note that Peter Pentz, the famous Indian fighter, killed a *maned* male panther near McElhattan Run, Clinton County, in 1798. The Indians told the Dutch settlers on Manhattan Island that the hides of panthers they brought there to sell were from females, that the males had manes and were difficult to capture. Perhaps the earliest form of the panther possessed maned males. They may be a modification of the prehistoric lions which Prof. Leidy called *felis atrox*, and which ranged parts of the continent. The Indians may have repeated an old tradition, and not something made out of the whole cloth. Panthers lived in shallow caves along the steep slopes of the rockier of the Pennsylvania mountains. Peter Pentz, it is said, crawled into a deep cavern to kill the maned panther and its mate. George Shover blocked up a panther in a cave on Little Miller Run, Lycoming County, in 1865, built a fire and suffocated the beast. There have been a few Pennsylvanians who called the Pennsylvania lion the cougar, and a still smaller number who alluded to it as the puma. There has been a wide range to the scientific nomenclature. S. N. Rhoads, the Philadelphia naturalist, who knows more about the panther than any other man in the State, gives preference to *felis couguar*. This is undoubtedly superior to *felis concolor*, which conveys very little. Others have referred to it as the American Lion, Brown Tiger and Catamount. The last title refers more properly to the

Canada Lynx, or big grey wild cat. The Pennsylvania Germans used to call the panther the Bender. Philip Tome, in his "Thirty Years a Hunter," tells of Rice Hamlin killing a panther on the Tiadaghton weighing 200 pounds. About 115 pounds was a good average weight for a mature Pennsylvania Lion. Tome, who also was probably the greatest of all Pennsylvania hunters of big game, has recorded many of his hunting adventures in a book entitled "Thirty Years a Hunter." He was a sportsman as well as hunter, never killing recklessly. Though he makes no recapitulation of panthers which fell to his unerring bullets, his descendants estimate that he killed at least 500 of these noble animals. One of his grandsons, George L. Tome, a noted hunter, resides at Corydon, in Warren County. Old Mifflin County hunters described a panther killed by John Reager and William Dellett near Milroy in 1869 as being so large that when the carcass was thrown across the shoulders of a horse the head dragged on one side and the tail on the other. According to the Pennsylvania hunters the specimens of *felis couguar* now seen in Zoological gardens have faded coats, or else the western individuals are plainer colored. It is said that the winter sunlight shining on the many tinted coats of the Pennsylvania lion was a sight beautiful to behold. Even in death the hides retain the rich fulvous, fawn, orange and lemon tints for forty years or more. George G. Hastings vividly describes a magnificent male panther which sunned itself and

rolled in the snow on the breast of a splash dam on
Big Run, Centre County, in February, 1872, when he
was alone and unarmed at a nearby camp. The great
feline seemed to be aware of the Nimrod's *unpre-
paredness,* lingering about the premises for upwards
of an hour. A Florida panther killed near Miami
in the winter of 1914, measures, length of head and
body 56 inches, length of tail 28 inches. The hide was
sent to the writer by the naturalist Rhoads. It rep-
resents the extreme peninsular dark phase, being a
rich chocolate brown in color. The head is small, as
is the head of the West Virginia panther, previously
alluded to; the coat of the West Virginia specimen
is a paler brown, lacking much of the richness of the
Florida hide. A dark dorsal line from shoulders to
tip of tail is very noticeable on the Florida specimen,
but like the West Virginia hide it has the tuft at end
of tail. A mounted Florida panther in the Museum of
Natural History, New York City, is a sooty, or slate
grey in color, very different from the hide procured
by Mr. Rhoads.

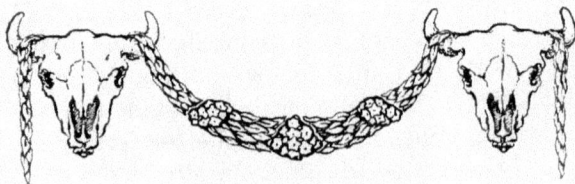

IV. HABITS.

I T is unfortunate that when the Pennsylvania lion
was prevalent no local naturalists made an at-
tempt to study the habits of the noble animal. Mr.
S. N. Rhoads, in his "Mammals of Pennsylvania and
New Jersey," gives us the most complete account, but it
was written years after the animal's disappearance and
mostly from hearsay evidence. In the first place, the
panther of Pennsylvania was not "unnecessarily
cruel." It fed mostly on decrepit and wounded deer
and elk, sickly game birds and rabbits, also on mice,
rats, bugs, worms and berries. It was also a scavenger,
eating animals which had died after receiving wounds
from hunters, and those which had succumbed from
natural causes. In a forest it was a decidedly benefi-
cial element. It never killed more than it could eat
under any circumstances. There is no authentic case
of the Pennsylvania lion having attacked human beings
even when wounded. There is a story prevalent in
Lycoming County of a doctor having been eaten by a
panther about 1840; later researches prove that he was
lost in the snow and died of exposure. Wolves, panthers and hawks picked his carcass, not knowing
enough to respect a human corpse, but that was the
very worst. D. S. Maynard, in his "Historical View
of Clinton County," published in 1874, tells of an occasion when the workmen on the State Road between
Renovo and Germania found the bones of a man "who

no doubt had been killed and eaten by a panther."
Probably the man died from exposure, and his carcass
was chewed up by the lion. The same author men-
tions an instance near Young Woman's Town, now
North Bend, where a panther killed and devoured an
ox, and another instance where a panther killed a
fox, which, jackal fashion, had been following it to
obtain a share of the "swag." Another case, on Pine
Creek, on the Clinton County shore, is that of a child
going after the cows, which had to pass under an
overhanging timber of an abandoned dam, on which
a panther was crouched, and the brute springing on
the child devoured it. This was supposed to have
happened about 1820, but no names are obtainable.
The child was probably lost in the woods or kidnaped
by the Indians who camped at the mouth of the creek
When wounded, panthers courageously attacked the
dogs, but refused to molest hunters. When about to
be knifed or shot, these animals are known to have
looked the hunters in the eyes and shed real tears. It
is recorded that panthers made interesting and affec-
tionate pets. An admirer in Philadelphia sent a young
Pennsylvania lion to Edmund Kean, a celebrated Eng-
lish actor. It followed him about the streets of Lon-
don, attracting more attention than Alderman Parkin's
team of quaggas. D'Azara's tame panther is recorded
as being gentle, but very sluggish. Agnes Sorel, the
celebrated Parisian actress, was presented with a lively
young panther by a South American admirer. A short
time ago the lady presented the animal to the Jardin

des Plantes, where it can be seen and admired by multitudes. Several "pilots" on the West Branch of the Susquehanna kept panther cubs on their rafts, which were as playful as kittens. In Pennsylvania the rutting season usually occurred in December, and according to the old hunters, the period of gestation lasted three lunar months. Jack Long, the famous hunter in discussing the subject with Dr. W. J. McKnight, author of "Pioneer Outline History of Northwestern Pennsylvania," said that panthers brought forth their young in September. Audubon says gestation took 97 days, and Dr. Conklin, former director of Central Park Zoological Garden, New York City, claims 91 days as the period. Three to six pups was the number of young produced by Pennsylvania panthers. Jesse Logan, Indian panther hunter, says that panther cubs were delicate, and many died while teething. Audubon says there have been instances of five at a birth, in speaking of the species in general. Samuel Askey, the great Centre county panther slayer, obtained four pups in a nest on more than one occasion. In 1871 Calvin Wagner, of Bannerville, Snyder county, when crossing the Seven Mountains near Zerby, found a pantheress stretched out across the path, playing with six healthy looking pups. He was unarmed, and as the panthers made no move to vacate, he took a detour to pass them. Hurrying down the mountain he obtained a rifle from a settler near Penn's Creek, and returned to the spot, but the animals were nowhere to be seen. On the return, he encountered a

herd of about thirty deer, another unusual occurrence
for that time. The young panthers usually followed
the mother until almost full grown. They hunted
with her, but when two or three years old left to seek
mates. Panthers did not have young every year, but
only brought forth a fresh litter when abandoned by
their almost mature offspring. In "Fur News Magazine" a writer from Perry County describes a battle to
the death between male panthers which was witnessed
one night by a belated traveler crossing the "Seven
Brothers," as the Seven Mountains, the Tussey, Path
Valley, Thick Head, Sand, Bald, Shade and Stone
ranges, are often called. The traveler watched the com-
bat from behind a big rock, seeing the two fierce brutes
tear each other to pieces. The males and females,
except mother and young, kept separate except during
the mating season. The panther is a silent animal
except at this season, and when its young is taken.
Its love song was majestic, but its cry of maternal
anguish one of the most doleful to be conjured by the
imagination. W. H. Schwartz, the brilliant editor of
the Altoona Tribune, recently wrote: "Anent the cry
of the panther. This writer had many conversations
with a gentleman who was born in 1768 and who was
one of the pioneers in this vicinity. Many times did
he make our young blood run cold by the tales of the
panther and its habit of crying through the night like
an abandoned child. More than that, the writer, some
sixty-two years ago, heard a plaintive cry one night
as he spent the night with his grandmother, near

Canoe Creek, and was assured by her that it was a
panther. The cry was repeated several times."
Panthers were fond of standing erect when sharpening their claws against the rough bark of the tupelo
trees. Franklin Shreckengast relates how two hunters
on Baker's Run, in Centre county, in an early day
carved away a section of bark from one of these trees
and cut on the smooth surface "Dec. 4, 1858, Jake
Hall, Abe Glelson, kilt 4 deers heer." The tupelo in
question was a favorite nail sharpening resort of the
panthers which trailed the aged or wounded deer in
that section and shortly afterwards with their heavy
claws the huge brutes completely effaced the boastful
record of the enterprising Nimrods.

That the panther would resent meddling is attested
to by George Huff, born in 1835, of White Deer,
Union County, who tells how a man named Jacob
Lushbaugh, a hunter in the White Deer Mountains,
in trying to rescue a favorite dog from the grip of a
panther had one of his hands badly lacerated by the
monster's fangs.

V. EARLY PREVALENCE.

LIONS in British East Africa were never more prevalent than was the panther in Pennsylvania a century or more ago. The woods fairly teemed with them. Yet they made no inroads on the myriads of elk, deer, hares, heath-cocks, wild turkeys, grouse, quails, wild pigeons, rabbits and hares which shared the forest covers with them. The first settlers destroyed all game mercilessly and when it grew scarce blamed its disappearance on the panthers, lynxes, wildcats, wolves and foxes. A warfare was waged against the miscalled predatory beasts; they were exterminated, but game became scarcer than ever. It is now only that people are beginning to wake up to the fact that the panthers were the victims of a cowardly plot to avert the white hunters' culpability. S. N. Rhoads states that in Luzerne county bounties amouning to $1,822 were paid on the scalps of panthers between 1808 and 1820. More than fifty of these superb animals were killed in one year. J. J. Audubon relates that "Among the mountains of the headwaters of the Juniata river, as we were informed, the cougar is so abundant that one man has killed for some years from two to five, and one very hard winter seven." This was written about 1850. Samuel Askey, of Snow Shoe. Centre county, killed sixty-four panthers between the years of 1820 and 1845. These

24

were taken in a limited district and all of this great
hunter's neighbors were engaged slaying panthers at
the same time. During these twenty-five years it is
estimated that six hundred panthers were killed in
Centre county. Eleven full grown panthers were
killed on Medix Run, which flows through Clearfield
and Elk counties, during the winter of 1853. At no
time, however, was the range of the Pennsylvania lion
evenly distributed. While it was teeming in Centre.
Clearfield and counties further South, it was a rare
visitor in Potter, McKean and Warren counties.
C. W. Dickinson, the great hunter of the Black Forest.
says: "Panthers were never as prevalent at the headwaters of the Alleghany as on the Susquehanna, the
Clarion, or the Juniata. I don't believe that more
than ten or twelve were captured in what is now Mc-
Kean county since the first white man settled there.
I believe that panthers, like wild cats, were afraid of
the *grey* timber wolves which abounded there. Yet
the panther was almost as plentiful in Tioga, Bradford
and Susquehanna counties as it was in Centre or
Mifflin. Hundreds were slain in Susquehanna county
and Blackman's history of that county abounds with
instances of its appearance among the early settlers.
It was killed by the hundreds in Wyoming and counties directly South. It bred in the inaccessible swamps
in Susquehanna county and among the rocky fast-
nesses at the headwaters of the Lehigh river. It was
never plentiful in Clinton county, but was found in
great numbers in Lycoming and Sullivan. The lim-

ited range and the limited amount of wild territory in
Pennsylvania set an early doom on the native lions.
Gradually civilization closed in, and the number of
hunters increased yearly. Panther hides were as prevalent on the walls of old-time farm buildings as
woodchuck skins are today. Almost every backwoods
kitchen had a panther coverlet on the lounge by the
stove. Panther tracks could be seen crossing and re-
crossing all the fields, yet children on their way to
school were never molested. In an early day in Centre
county hunters who had killed fifty panthers were of no
rare occurrence. Among the Jefferson county hunters
who killed fifty panthers may be mentioned "Bill" Long,
"The King Hunter," who died in May, 1880, in his
ninety-first year. Young bloods dared not pay
court to a girl unless they could boast of having killed
a panther or two. Even preachers and missionaries
joined in the chase and some of them held high scores
in the awful game of slaughter. Panthers insisted in
returning to spots where they had reared their young
the season before. The hunters were soon aware
of the panther "ledges" or clefts" and robbed them
annually. They lay in wait for the old animals, killing them without quarter. A dog which would not
trail a panther was held to be of small value. Tame
panthers were used to attract their wild relatives out
of the forests. Joseph McConnel, a pioneer in
Northern Juniata county, killed eleven panthers in
seven years in this way. He is said to have
covered one entire side of his barn with panther

hides. He thought so little of them that they
rotted where they hung and were blown apart by
heavy gales. German buyers secured many panther
skins, as there was a steady demand in the "old country" for these hides, like there always has been for
walnut. Schroeder & Co., of Lock Haven, sent their
last consignment to Germany in 1893. William Perry
killed a mature male panther on Yost Run, Centre
county, in 1875, which was seen in the trap by S. A.
Wadsworth and J. A. Roan, residents of Clinton county, now living. Roan says that the animal's head was
covered with old scars, showing where it had been in
sanguinary battles with rivals in the past. James
Wylie Miller, veteran hunter of Clinton county, but
formerly of Cameron county, killed many deer in the
old days the flanks of which had been scarred by
panthers in their ineffectual efforts to. bring them
down. On one occasion Miller saw the tracks of nine
panthers on a "crossing" on Up Jerry Run, in Cameron county. In Miller's boyhood days, he was born
in 1838, the greatest panther hunters in the Sinnemahoning Valley were Joe Berfield, John Jordan, Arch
Logue and Henry Mason, who resided a short distance up the East Fork. According to Jonas J.
Barnet, born in 1838, of Weikert, Union County,
panthers were so prevalent on Penn's Creek in the
first decade of the Nineteenth Century that his uncle,
Jacob Weikert, was unable to keep pigs for a period
of seven years. Mary Hironimus, of Weikert, was
followed four miles by a panther; the experience

made her an invalid for nearly a year, as the huge
cat treated her as a "Tabby" would a mouse, letting
her walk along the path a few feet ahead of him, stop-
ping when she stopped and running when she ran.
Mrs. Mary De Long, of Stover's, in Brush Valley,
Centre county, in walking along a forest path saw a
panther crouched above her on the limb of a large
white oak, but the animal suffered her to pass beneath.
On another occasion at night, when going for help
when her mother was ill, she met a panther by the
path. By holding the lantern between herself and
the monster she was allowed to go her way, the
panther keeping abreast of her just far enough in the
shadows to avoid the light, until she reached the
neighbor's cabin. The fear of panthers was so firmly
implanted in her that her descendants to this day
always instinctively look up in the forks of large trees
when passing through a forest. Panthers often
leaped on roofs of shanties at night, frightening the
female occupants considerably. John S. Hoar tells of
an instance of this kind in Treaster Valley (Mifflin
County) about 1896, and another similar occurrence
is recorded in Miss Blackman's "History of Susquehanna County."

VI.   THE GREAT SLAUGHTER.

A NIMAL drives, similar to those once held in South Africa, were as plentiful in Central and Southern Pennsylvania as in the "Northern tier." As they occurred in the remote backwoods districts where no written history was kept, accounts of them have well-nigh lapsed into oblivion. One of the greatest drives ever known took place about 1760, in the vicinity of Pomfret Castle, a fort for defense against the Indians, which had been constructed in 1756. "Black Jack" Schwartz was the leader of this drive, which resulted in the death of more than forty panthers. Schwartz, or as he is often called, "The Wild Hunter of the Juniata," must not be confounded with Captain Jack Armstrong, a trader, who was murdered by Indians in Jack's Narrows in 1744. History has confused the two men, but as the wild hunter offered his command of sharpshooters to Gen. Braddock in 1755 there can be no doubt that they were different persons. Panthers and wolves had been troubling the more timid of the settlers, and a grand drive towards the centre of a circle thirty miles in diameter was planned. A plot of ground was cleared into which the animals were driven. In the outer edge of the circle fires were started, guns fired, bells rung, all manner of noises made. The hunters, men and boys, to the number of two hundred, gradually closed in on the centre. When they reached the point where the killing was to be made, they found it crowded with yelping, growling, bellowing animals. Then the slaughter began, not ending until the last animal had been slain. A group of Buffaloes broke through the guards at an early stage of the killing, and it is estimated that several hundred animals escaped in this way. The recapitulation is as follows, the count having been made by Black Jack himself at the close of the carnage: Forty-one panthers, 109 wolves, 112 foxes, 114 mountain cats, 17 black bears, 1 white bear, 2 elk, 198 deer, 111 buffaloes, 3 fishers, 1 otter, 12 gluttons, 3 beavers and upwards of 500 smaller animals. The percentage of panthers to the entire number killed is an interesting commentary on the early prevalence of these animals. The choicest hides were taken, together with buffalo tongues, and then the heap of carcasses "as tall as the tallest trees," was heaped with rich pine and fired. This created such a stench that the settlers were compelled to vacate their cabins in the vicinity of the fort, three miles away. There is a small mound, which on being dug into is filled with bones, that marks the spot of the slaughter, near the head waters of (West) Mahantango Creek. Black Jack's unpopularity with the Indians was added to when they learned of this animal drive. The red men, who only killed such animals as they actually needed for furs and food, and were real conservationists, resented such a wholesale butchery. The story goes that the wild hunter was ambushed by Indians while on a hunting trip and killed. Animal drives did not cease with Black Jack's death, but in some localities they were held annually, until game became practically exterminated. They were held in Northern Pennsylvania, which was settled at a much later date, until about 1830. After the great slaughter of Pomfret Castle, many backwoodsmen appeared in full suits of panther skin. For several years they were known as the "Panther Boys," and in their old days they delighted to recount the "big hunt" to their descendants. Among those said to have taken part in it were Jack Schwartz, Michael Dougherty, Felix Delehanty, Terence McGuire, Patt. Mitcheltree, brother of Hugh Mitcheltree, who was carried off by six Indians in 1756; Abraham Hart, Michael Flinn and Isaac Delaplain. The panther uniforms were abandoned because they became favorite targets for skulking Indians. The savages, infuriated by the arrogance of the white newcomers, spared persons falling into their power occasionally, but gave no quarter to a "Panther Boy." The great slaughter of animals kept alive ill feeling between the two races in the region of the Firestone Mountains, and probably a dozen settlers lost their lives because of it. However, they went on with their animal drives, as the hardy settlers loved to do what the Indians hated. Of all the hunters contributing to the final extermination of the Pennsylvania lion, Aaron Hall, who died at his palatial mansion back of Unionville, Centre county, in 1892, stands well up on the list. Between the years 1845 and 1869 he killed fifty panthers, principally in Centre and Clearfield counties. As he began his career as a hunter on Bell's and Tipton runs, tributaries of the Juniata, he was often called the "Lion Hunter of the Juniata." On one occasion when visited by Hon. C. K. Sober, of Lewisburg, former State Game Commissioner, he had the hides of eleven panthers hanging up at his camp on Rock Run. In 1849 the last animal drive or "Ring Hunt" was held by the Pioneers at Beech Creek, Clinton county. Several panthers, it is said, escaped through the human barrier.

VII. THE BIGGEST PANTHER.

WITH practically no written records it is well nigh impossible to gain a correct idea of the general size of Pennsylvania panthers. As far as it is known there are three mounted panthers in existence, one at State College, one at Albright College and a third at McElhattan. In addition to these the writer possesses four hides of panthers, two killed by Aaron Hall, two by George G. Hastings. The first named mounted specimen, a male, killed by Samuel E. Brush in Susquehanna county in 1856, measures 7 feet 9 inches; the second, also a male, killed by Lewis Dorman in Centre county in 1868, is 8 feet; the third, a female, killed by Thomas Anson in Berks county in 1874, is 6 feet 6 inches from tip to tip. This would give a fair average of the sizes. One of the largest Pennsylvania panthers on record taken in recent years was killed in Clinton county, on Young Woman's Creek, by Sam Snyder, on January 5, 1857. It measured a few hours after it was shot, nine feet two inches. This giant animal had been heard running the deer along the ridges near the creek for several weeks, and several parties had been organized to capture it. It remained for Sam Snyder, a lad of twenty years, with his pack of six trained fices, to run it down. One bright morning he tracked it to a point where it was forced to take refuge on an overhanging

branch of a mammoth white oak. He fired at it, the
bullet passing through its left shoulder. The wound
served to infuriate the monster, and it leaped from the
tree, landing in the centre of the snarling, snapping
pack of dogs. Backing up against the butt of a fallen
hemlock, with its right paw, which was not disabled, it
killed five of the fices before the hunter sent a bullet
into its brain. The fice which escaped was a tiny ter-
rier, which was alert enough to keep out of reach of
the brute's paw. The huge carcass was transported in
an ox-cart to Young Woman's Town, now North
Bend, where after it hung for a day in front of a tav-
ern, it was skinned and the hide sold to Matthew
Hanna, Jr., a hotel keeper of Young Woman's Town.
The carcass was cut up into roasts and steaks, and
the entire settlement feasted on it for several days.
One dark night, ten years later, Jacob K. Huff, better
known as "Faraway Moses," was followed down
Young Woman's Creek by a panther. The brute kept
along the side of the ridge, howling every few minutes, until it neared the settlement. Evidently the
panther had young, and feared that the traveler might
molest them. James E. DeKay, in his Natural History of New York State, described a panther killed
by Joe Wood at Fourth Lake of Fulton Chain, in
Herkimer county, New York, which measured eleven
feet three inches. The stuffed hide was exhibited for
many years at the Utica Museum. The contents of
this Museum were removed, it is stated, to Jackson-
ville, Florida, about 1870. "Adirondack" Murray,

writing about 1869, says that the panther of the "North Woods" often measured twelve feet from tip to tip. Simon Pfouts, of Leidy township, Clinton county, caught a record panther in a trap near the mouth of Beaver Dam run which measured eleven feet six inches from tip to tip. This is mentioned in Maynard's "Historical View of Clinton County." Dr. Merriam believes eight feet to be a good average size. This would indicate a close similarity in dimensions between the panthers of the Adirondacks, Pennsylvania and the West. Colonel Roosevelt killed six cougars in Colorado in 1901 which averaged a trifle over eight feet apiece. If anything the Pennsylvania panthers, like the Pennsylvania trees, were larger on the average than those of the Adirondacks. It was the ideal location for them to thrive, for as Prof. J. A. Allen said: "The maximum physical development of the individual is attained where the conditions of environment are most favorable to the life of the species." The panthers which George G. Hastings, of Buffalo Run, Centre county, killed on December 30 and 31, 1871, measured nine feet and eight feet nine inches, respectively. The larger was the female, and Mr. Hastings believed it was the mother of the smaller one. George Shover killed a giant male panther on Little Miller Run, Lycoming county, in January, 1865, which measured eleven feet from tip to tip. For some reason male panthers were much more numerous in Pennsylvania than female. The opposite was the case in the Adirondacks, according to Dr. Merriam. Of all the instances of panthers noted by the writer of this article, not more than six at most, were females. The information concerning Sam Snyder's record panther was given to the writer by John G. Davis, of McElhattan, who moved to Young Woman's Town with his parents in April of the year in which the beast was killed. He was sixteen years old at the time and remembers the details of the occurrence vividly. Michael Pluff, who died at Hyner, Clinton county, in January, 1914, aged 74 years, also recalled the circumstance. It is recorded at length in Maynard's History of the County. Hon. J. W. Crawford, of North Bend. Pa., published an interesting account of this panther in the "Renovo Record" of February 20, 1914. He says that Snyder went to the front in 1861 and was killed at Fort Sumter. The story is well known in Clinton and adjoining counties and several persons, including Judge Crawford, who saw the panther when it was brought to Young Woman's Town, are still "in the land of the living." The world of sport hails Sam Snyder as a mighty Nimrod! Simon Pfouts, the great hunter, was the first white man to settle on Kettle Creek, Clinton county. At the foot of Spicewood Island he found, on one occasion, three young panthers lying in their nest of leaves underneath the shelter of an old root. He quickly gathered them up in his arms and started home. When he had arrived within one-fourth of a mile of his residence the sound of panther yells fell upon his ears. Then commenced a race for life, and Pfouts fully de-

veloped the strength of his muscles. Nearer and
nearer were the screams of the huge monster. Pfouts
gained the race by a few feet, and rushing into the
house he dropped the young panthers and seizing his
rifle shot the panther, which fell dead near his door.
On another occasion, in company with Paul Shade,
pushing a canoe up the river laden with provisions,
when within a mile or two of his home, at a point
where the channel of the stream is narrow, suddenly
an enormous panther leaped from his concealed posi-
tion among the rocks at the form of Pfouts, and
alighted in the water close to the stern of the canoe, the
rapid current carrying it some distance down stream
before it reached shore. One day, while out hunting
with his well-trained dogs, he killed four panthers,
and the following day he killed another. Meshach
Browning, in his entertaining work entitled "Forty-
four Years a Hunter" (first published in Philadelphia
in 1865), thus describes the killing of a record panther
in the Maryland Mountains, near the Pennsylvania
line:

"Not long after we had settled in our new home,
there fell a light snow, when I took my rifle, and, calling a dog which I had brought with me from Wheel-
ing, which was of the stock of old Mr. Caldwell's
hunting dogs, I went into the woods after deer. I had
not traveled far before I found the tracks of four
deer, which had run off; for they had got wind of me,
and dashed into a great thicket to hide themselves. I
took the trail, and into the thicket I went, where I

soon saw the deer running in different directions. I
got between them, in hopes that I should see them
trying to come together again. I kept my stand perhaps five or six minutes, when I saw something slip-
ping through the bushes, which I took to be one of
the deer; but I soon found that it was coming toward
me. I kept a close look out for it; and directly, within
ten steps of me, up rose the head and shoulders of the
largest panther that I ever saw, either before or since.
He kept behind a large log that was near me, and
looked over. But though I had never seen a wild one
before, I knew the gentleman, and was rather afraid
of him. I aimed my rifle at him as well as I could, he
looking me full in the face; and when I fired he made
a tremendous spring from me, and ran off through the
brush and briars, with the dog after him.

"As soon as I recovered a little from my fright I
loaded again, and started after them. I followed them
as fast as I could, and soon found them at the foot
of a large and very high rock; the panther, in his
hurry, having sprung down the cleft of rock fifteen
or twenty feet; but the dog, being afraid to venture
so great a leap, ran around, and the two had met in a
thick laurel swamp, where they were fighting the
best way they could, each trying to get the advantage
of the other. I stood on the top of the rock over them,
and fired at the base of the panther's ear, when down
he went; and I ran round the rock, with my toma-
hawk in hand, believing him to be dead. But when I
got near him, I found he was up and fighting again,

and consequently I had to hurry back for my gun, load it again, creep slyly up, take aim at his ear, as before, and give him another shot, which laid him dead on the ground. My first shot had broken his shoulder; the second pierced his ear, passing downward through his tongue; the last entered one ear, and came out at the other, scattering his brains all around. He measured eleven feet three inches from the end of his nose to the tip of his tail. This was the largest panther I ever killed, and I suppose I have killed at least fifty in my time.

"I took from this fellow sixteen and a half pounds of rendered tallow. It is something softer than mutton tallow, but by mixing it with one-fourth of its weight of beeswax, it makes good candles. I continued hunting the balance of the season, with little success —not killing any bears, although there were great numbers of them in the woods. However, I knew but little of the art of hunting." A panther killed by John Treaster in the Seven Mountains in 1875 measured, body and head 8 feet, tail 3 feet, total eleven feet, almost the record. Dr. Schoepf describes a shrunken hide of a South Carolina panther as "over five foot from the muzzle to beginning of tail, the tail itself somewhat more than three feet long; the back and sides and head fallow, nearly fawn colored, flanks and belly whitish grey; the end of tail verged somewhat on black, but the rest of the tail was of the color of the body."

VIII. DIMINISHING NUMBERS.

WITH the hand of all raised against them, it is small wonder that by 1860 the panther had become a rarity in the Pennsylvania wilds. Three or four were the most killed in any one year from that date on, until the final extermination. After 1860, they bred in but two localities in the Commonwealth—in the Divide Region of Clearfield County, in Mifflin County. In Clearfield County they had the widest range, and increased most satisfactorily. There was an almost impenetrable evergreen forest at the head of Medix Run, which did not first feel the woodman's axe until 1904, and which was a panther's paradise. A few panthers bred there until about 1892. The cries of panthers and the howling of wolves could be heard there for a few years after that. Sam Odin, of Clifford, Susquehanna County, killed the last panther in the northern section in February, 1874. It is described as having ben a superb male, red colored and weighing 153 pounds. Its measurements are not given. A female which was with it escaped, and is probably the same one which was killed by Thomas Anson, a coal-burner on the slope of the Pinnacle, in Northern Berks County, in August of that year, according to O. D. Shock, now of the Public Service Commission at Harrisburg. "Forest and Stream" (Vol. III, Page 67) gives the weight of this animal as 146 pounds,

length 6 feet 5½ inches. Measured in the study of
the writer of this article, where it now reposes, it is
exactly six feet six inches! The old hunters were not
all "gross exaggerators," as some would have us
think. The story of the killing of this panther is of
more than passing interest. The coal-burners lived in
a shack on the east face of the Pinnacle, which is the
highest point in Berks County. Nearby is the celebrated "Amphitheatre," where the Blue Mountains
appear to form a horseshoe about the village of Eckville and its surrounding fields. Travelers have com-
pared it to the "Cirque de Gavarnie" in the Pyrenees.
On several nights the coal-burners heard the animal
prowling about their premises, much to the terror of
their dogs. They supposed it to be a wild cat, as these
animals were very plentiful in the neighborhood. One
evening Jacob Pfleger, one of the burners, went to a
farmhouse to get a pan of butter. It was dusk when
he started for the shack, but he was able to observe
that he was being followed by a huge cat-like animal.
He kept his nerve, and was gratified to find that the
monster ceased following him when it reached a large
spring. There it began lapping up the water like a cat.
He was unarmed, but at the shanty he found one of
his companions, Thomas Anson, who owned a rifle.
Anson is said to have killed a panther in Wayne County—the last known in that section—in 1867. The two
men returned to the spring, finding the panther not far
distant. Anson put several bullets into the brute's
body, ending its life. To this day the spring has been

known as "The Panther Spring." It is a fine pool of
water, and is along the mountain road between Wind-
sor Furnace and Eckville. A sketch was made of the
spring by Artist C. H. Shearer in August, 1912. How
this panther wandered into Berks County, where none
of its kind had been seen in forty years, can only be ex-
plained by the fact that the creature was working its
way westward in search of a mate. Faires Boyer, a
noted hunter, residing at Centreville, Snyder County,
killed a panther on Jack's Mountain in November,
1873. It had been probably driven eastward by dogs.
Clement F. Herlacher killed two panthers on Mos-
quito Creek, in Clearfield County, in February, 1880.
For many nights they had been annoying the horses
at a big camp, the frightened animals prancing and
foaming while the panthers prowled outside. Leonard
Johnson, of McElhattan, Clinton County, remembers
this incident very well. The panthers in Treaster
Valley did little damage, and were in a sense protected
by the old settlers, who resented "outsiders" hunting
or cruising about the valley. Even Dr. Rothrock was
warned to be "careful" in passing through the valley
alone. Clem Herlacher followed these panthers by
their regular "crossing" from Sugar Valley, Clinton
County, and discovered their "ledge," in the early
summer of 1892. He abstracted four pups, which
were about three or four months old. Returning the
following year, he found two pups in the same nest,
which he also carried away. Many of the old hunters
believed that in some mysterious way the Pennsylva-

nia lion, like the wolf, was an integral part of the orig-
inal forest. When the old forests were cut, the panthers and wolves of the Keystone State diminished,
until the destruction of practically all of the "first
growth" timber, they vanished altogether. This may
also account for the passing of panthers and wolves
from the Adirondack Mountains in New York, which
occurred so completely after the lumbermen's devas-
tation.

IX. THE LAST PHASE.

A ND now the noble lion of Pennsylvania is re-
duced to a mere foot-print, a voice, a memory
of other days. He is spoken of by persons who
have heard rather than seen him. William J. Emert,
of Youngdale, Clinton County, whose fish basket was
rifled by a wandering panther at his bark camp near
Dagusgahonda, Elk County, in 1889, remembers the
animal's cries distinctly, and can give an exhibition of
unique mimicry. The writer, having heard the cries
of the panther in a wild state and in capitivity, can
vouch for it that the genial Bill actually heard the real
thing. Potter County newspapers in 1911 reported
that the cries of a panther were heard in the vicinity
of Sweden Hill, near Coudersport, in the autumn of
that year. The same fall a panther was heard near
Bare Meadows, Centre County, some nights roaring
from the very summit of Bald Top. When calling
for their mates they invariably climbed to the highest
peaks. This panther was tracked during a light snow
fall clear to Stone Valley. Some say that it was killed
there. Franklin Shreckengast, of Tylersville, Clinton
County, on commenting on the volume of the panther's
cry, said: "If a panther roared on the other side of
the Nittany Mountain, all Sugar Valley would be
aroused tonight." Shreckengast, who is now in his
78th year, hunted panthers with the Askey boys near

44

Snow Shoe, Centre County, during the Civil War. James Lebo, of Lucullus, Lycoming County, tracked two panthers across his fields in February, 1909. They were traveling in a northeasterly direction. During the summer of that year panther cries were heard at different points along the Coudersport pike, which runs past the Lebo home. Across the road from this gentleman's residence is the swale where the mangled body of little Edna Cryder was found in 1896. Panther tracks were observed on the Pike by Dr. Rothrock in 1913; in Detwiler Hollow, in the Seven Mountains, in the same year, by several hunters. In November, 1912, three rabbit hunters scared up a panther which was sleeping under the prostrate top of a pine tree, in Detwiler. In November, 1913, several farmers heard panther cries, and one reliable person saw a panther in his barnyard in Logan Valley, near Altoona. Johns- town papers reported a panther as doing much damage to deer and other game on Laurel Ridge, in Somerset County, in the same month. There is probably a panther path leading into Pennsylvania from the Maryland and West Virginia Mountains. This is proved by the killing of a panther in November, 1913, several miles north of Washington, D. C. This wanderer evidently heard or scented the mountain lions at Rocky Creek Park Zoo, lost his bearings, became overconfident and paid the death penalty. The path must lead up the Laurel Ridge to Blue Knob, where it diverges, one line heading north through Centre County to Potter County, the other northeast along the Bald

Eagle Mountain to the Tussey Mountains, thence into
the Seven Mountains country. Hon. C. K. Sober says
that he feels confident that panthers still come into
Pennsylvania by these paths. Panthers had a regular
crossing from Nittany Valley to the Summit country
at Hoppleton, Clinton County; thence across Sugar
Valley, and from there south to Treaster Valley, Mifflin County, where they bred. Emmanuel Harman,
as a boy, encountered panthers on this crossing, while
A. D. Karstetter, Postmaster at Loganton, can recall
panthers crossing Sugar Valley within the past thirty
years. The panther which Wilson Rishel heard on the
Sugar Valley Mountain, south of Tylersville, Clinton
County, in 1870, was heard the day previously at
Lamar, and the day before that in the east end of
Nittany Valley, according to Dr. Jonathan Moyer.
Emmanuel Harman heard the same panther the week
before in Gottshall Hollow. David Mark, born in
1835, says that panthers were always a rare animal in
Sugar Valley, only passing through there at intervals
by their regular paths. The Seven Mountains was the
last stand of the native panthers in Pennsylvania.
Clement F. Herlacher camped in Treaster Valley in
the summers of 1892 and 1893, as has been stated previously, having heard rumors that the pair of panthers which he tracked to the valley were breeding
there. As the result he captured four cubs in 1892
and two the following year, but the old ones escaped.
He says the old panthers "took on" terribly over the
loss of their young. It was probably these unhappy

creatures which Dr. J. T. Rothrock, of West Chester, heard during his visit to this valley in 1893. His description of the panther's cry, which we give in chapter XI, is to natural history what Abraham Lincoln's Gettysburg speech is to oratory; it surely is the pearl without price. Although the good doctor is now in his 78th year, his mastery of diction is unimpaired. One can feel the clear, cold night, with the effulgent moon above all, and see the ragged outline of the Seven Mountains silhouetted against the cloudless heavens; one can feel the oppressive stillness uninterrupted by the stirring of a single twig until the panther's song begins. And that song, that terrible song, so filled with anguish, a banshee-like song, lamenting the passing of the wilderness, of the brute's supremacy, the loss of cover, of young, of hope, of life itself threatened. It was both a requiem and a swan-song! Several persons claim to have seen panthers in their old haunts on Rock Run, Centre County, during the past five years. A seven foot panther was reported killed during "deer season," 1915, near Paddy Mountain, Union County, but the report was later denied. Many persons claim to have heard and seen a panther on the Condersport Pike, near Haneyville, Clinton County, in 1913, 1914 and 1915. Residents of Treaster Valley report having seen panther tracks near the Panther Rocks, in that valley, in 1913 and 1914. Andy Wilson, guide and former game warden, now of Clinton County, saw a panther which approached his camp fire in the Seven Mountains in 1885. Hon. Frank B. Black,

former State Commissioner of Agriculture, and now
State Highway Commissioner, was followed by a
panther in Somerset County about the same year. In
about 1880, Hon. M. B. Rich, present member of the
Pennsylvania Legislature from Clinton County, was
followed by a panther on Little Pine Creek, Lycoming
County, for a distance of seven miles. H. Hollister,
in his "History of the Lackawanna Valley," tells of
being followed eight miles by a panther in 1837, in
Wayne County. Hollister was in a buggy at the
time, but the "Big Cat" could lope as fast as
the horse could gallop. C. E. "Doc" Smith, a
veteran Clinton County sportsman and naturalist,
saw panther tracks as big as a human hand on
Fish Dam Run, in the late seventies, when on a
hunting trip with Enoch Hastings. Davie Shaffer,
who worked in a lumber camp at the "Switches," in
Clinton County, near the panther's crossing, heard a
panther prowling around the shack one winter night
in 1880. Being alone, he built a big fire in front of
the cabin, sitting by it until daylight. Charles H.
Dyce, a successful lumber jobber, saw a panther on
the old Clay Pike which severely frightened his horse
Dewey, while returning to his home at Ebensburg
from his camp at Belsano, Cambria county, on the
evening of February 14, 1903. Early in 1914 the
carcass of an aged deer was found in the Seven
Mountains near Woodward that showed signs of having been killed and partly eaten by a panther.

X. RE-INTRODUCTION: SPORTING
POSSIBILITIES.

A S man becomes more educated, he will shrink
more and more each year from taking the lives
of tender, shrinking creatures like squirrels,
rabbits and quails. Many will hesitate from destroy-
ing gentle-eyed deer or the majestic elk. He will demand a quarry worthy of his status as a man, worthy
of his high-powered rifle. His mind will turn to larger
and more savage beasts, such as the red and black bear
and the panther. He will ask the re-introduction of
panthers and the adequate protection of bears. The
bear has its drawbacks on account of its hibernating
habits, its general lack of fighting qualities. He will
select the panther as his ideal of the big game animal.
The forest areas of Pennsylvania could be stocked
with these beasts and a five-year closed season put on
them to allow them to multiply. During this time these
subtle brutes would be well able to care for themselves.
They would feed on old and decrepid deer and elk,
sickly fawns, diseased hares and turkeys and in the
summer months on myriads of bugs, grubs, ants and
worms, and on roots and berries. Once the closed
season expired, sport royal would begin. There could
be an extra license charged for panther hunting, as the
territory and number of beasts being limited, it would
not be wise to have the forests overcrowded with hunt-

ers. Dr. C. Hart Merriam, in his intensely interesting
account of the animals of the Adirondack region, describes panther hunting as it was in the North Woods
thirty years ago. He says: "The hunter commonly
follows the panther for many days, and sometimes for
weeks, before overtaking him, and could never get him
were it not for the fact that he remains near the spot
where he kills a deer till it is eaten. When the hunter
has followed a panther for days, and has, perhaps,
nearly come up with him, a heavy snowstorm often
sets in and obliterates all signs of the track. He is
then obliged to make wide detours to ascertain in which
direction the animal has gone. On these long and tire-
some snowshoe tramps he is, of course, obliged to
sleep, without shelter, wherever night overtakes him.
The heavy walking makes it impossible for him to
carry many days' rations, and when his provision gives
out he must strike for some camp or settlement for a
new supply. This, of course, consumes valuable time
and enables the panther to get still further away.
When the beast is finally killed the event is celebrated
by a feast, for panther meat is not only paltable, but is
really fine eating." What grand, exhilarating, ennob-
ling sport it must have been! As practiced in the
Adirondacks, so it was carried on in Pennsylvania in
the old days. It is related that Lewis Dorman, a Centre county hunter, followed a panther for nearly two
months before he brought it to bay. Dorman, who was
a mighty hunter, died on November 28, 1905, and is
buried in St. Paul's Churchyard, near Woodward, in

John Penn's Valley. Henry Dorman, of Weikert, Union County, had occasion to carry a strip of bacon to a lumber camp on Cherry Run. It was at dusk, and a panther scenting the bacon, followed him the entire distance, occasionally howling mournfully. Packs of panther dogs would soon spring up in the mountainous settlements, and the breeding of these animals would give an impetus to the canine industry in these regions. Small bull dogs are said to be best for this purpose, though many prefer the ordinary whiffet or "fice." Aaron Hall, the "Lion Hunter of the Juniata," slayer of fifty panthers in Pennsylvania between 1845 and 1869, bred a race of panther dogs. They were part bull dog, part bloodhound, part Newfoundland, and part mastiff. They were so large that C. K. Sober, of Lewisburg, former State Game Commissioner, when on a visit to Hall at his hunting cabin on Rock Run, Centre County, was able to ride on the back of one of them. They were trained to hunt in pairs, and when the quarry was overtaken, to seize it by the ears on either side, holding the monster until the hunter appeared. With Hall's death, in 1892, this interesting breed of dog was allowed to become extinct. Old hunters declare there is nothing in the eating line that can equal a panther roast. It is said to taste like pork, only far more luscious in flavor. The meat is white like chicken, but of more substance. The hams are said to be superior to those of the hog. The panther hides are valuable as rugs, bed-covers and lap robes. The Seneca Indians made

the skin into pouches, in which they stored their "great
medicine." The claws were used as amulets to signify
the Indians' victory over the forces of evil, panthers
being supposed to have kinship to the Machtando or
Evil One. Panther oil was an efficacious remedy for
gall-stones and rheumatism. Hundreds of hunters—
among them Colonel Roosevelt—have been attracted to
Routt County, Colorado, by the panther hunting, where
these animals are trailed with dogs. Robert J. Collier,
a New York society man, headed a party of wealthy
hunters into this region in November, 1913, to hunt
"Mountain Lions." Colonel C. J. Jones has provided
similar sport for distinguished visitors at his ranch in
Arizona, the pastime there being to rope the "var-
mints." Pennsylvania can have all this and more, if
she will but set about to re-establish the superb sport.
In British East Africa, according to A. Barton Hep-
burn, of New York City, lions have been placed on
the protected list, the limit being four lions per hunter
a season. Why cannot Pennsylvania follow this ex-
cellent example and protect the Pennsylvania lion? It
is said that an old hunter named Noah Hallman, who
spent his last days near the Blue Mountain Amphitheatre in Northern Berks county, possessed several
trained panthers which he used to entice their wild
brethren out of the hiding places at the head waters
of the Lehigh River. Then the old Nimrod, who was
evidently an early prototype of Colonel Jones, would
lassoo the panthers and drag them back to his camp in
triumph.

XI. SUPERSTITIONS.

THERE has been a marked tendency with the latest generation of naturalists to belittle the entire race of *felis couguar*. Dr. Merriam, great man that he is, commenced it, and Colonel Roosevelt, by his article in "Scribner's Magazine" in 1901, fired the final gun. W. H. Hudson is the only naturalist who has spoken well of the species. It is the "style" to call the panther a coward, like has been done with the African lion. Why? Because he will not attack men. The African lion is said to charge when wounded, but the panther takes his medicine and dies like a gentleman. Dr. Merriam was the first to give popularity to the statement that there is no such thing as a panther cry, that it is all indigestion, imagination, superstitition on the part of the hunters, though in a letter to the author, dated March 24, 1914, this famous naturalist states that he referred solely to the panther of the Adirondacks. It may be possible that the Adirondack panther was a silent animal, but his relative in Pennsylvania was just the contrary. If, after the testimony of fifty hunters and old-timers whom the writer of this article has questioned on the subject are doubted, the following letter from Dr. J. T. Rothrock, founder of the Forestry Commission of Pennsylvania, and a scientist of world-wide reputation, should set the matter at rest for all time:

"WEST CHESTER, PA., JAN. 5. 1914.

DEAR MR. SHOEMAKER:

I have your very kind letter of January 2d. That panther cry—I have often asked myself how I could describe it and failed to satisfy the inquiry, though I think I have at this very minute a somewhat clear remembrance of it. It would not be an adequate reply if I said it sounded like the wail of a child seeking something, a cry, distinct, half inquiry and half in temper. There was something human in it, though unmistakably wild, clear and piercing. And yet I do not know how to make a more satisfactory reply, except to say that the cry seemed to be in all its tones about a minute long. I heard it one evening in Treaster Valley repeated so often that I could recognize it as coming from an animal moving along the rocky slope of the mountain where no child could have been at that hour, and was told by those residents in the region, 'Oh, it's the *painter's* cry.' It did not seem to be unusual to them. That was about twenty years ago.

Cordially yours,

(Signed) J. T. ROTHROCK."

Joseph H. Taylor, an able western writer on sporting topics, accurately describes the panther's cry which he heard during a flood at Lake Mandan, North Dakota, in March, 1880.

C. W. Dickinson says: "A great many writers claim that a panther does not scream or make any noise. They might as well try to make me believe that a pack of wolves could not howl or bark, growl or whine." Dickinson heard the panther cry at the head of the Driftwood branch of the Sinnemahoning when camping with his father, E. H. Dickinson, in the summer of 1872. He says it was "a loud, shrill, scream." He saw the last panther tracks on the Driftwood branch in January of the same year, while on a hunting trip with his father. But there are real superstitions of the painter—as most of the early settlers called it. It was said to have a very definite spirit, which came back and haunted familiar scenes after it had met with an unnatural death. A hunter in Centreville, Snyder county, in 1864, killed a large male panther, stuffed it and mounted it on the ridge-pole of his wood-house. One night the mate came after it, and springing on the roof, pushed the effigy into the yard. She carried it back to Jack's Mountain, where many persons averred it came to life again. In the White Mountains, not far from Troxelville, Snyder county, a panther was killed and its hide put into an attic to cure. Strange noises were heard, and the skin mounted on a carpenter's trestle was met with in the woods at night. A witch doctor hit the horrid manikin with a silver bullet, after which it gave no further trouble. Among the superstitious the Dorman panther was said to leave its case in the Natural History Museum on the top floor of the old Academy building at New Berlin on All Souls' Night and scamper about the big room after mice. It is now out of ghostly surroundings in the handsome new museum at Albright College, Myerstown, Lebanon County, having been taken there about 1905. Seneca Indians believed that the spirits of tyrants and unfaithful queens passed into panthers. They were hunted specifically for this and other before-mentioned reasons, having as little peace in animal form as in their human incarnations. Early German pioneers said that the panther's hide glowed like "fox-fire at night and green lights burned from the eyes." It was held to be good luck to be followed by a panther. It meant that outside forces were seeking the evil in the person followed, that it would soon be drawn away. Prof. E. Emmons, of Williams College, says in his Report on the Quadrupeds of Massachusetts: "The panther will not venture to attack man, yet it will follow his tracks a great distance; if it is near evening it frequently utters a scream which can be heard for miles." Some of the first Scotch-Irish frontiersmen regarded the panther's wailing as foretelling a death in the family. It was the "token" or "Banshee" of these sturdy souls. Samuel Stradley, a well-known hunter residing on the Tiadaghton or Pine Creek, in Lycoming County, while watching for deer at a crossing in 1870, fell asleep in the forest. When he awoke he found himself covered with leaves. Crawling out he sat perfectly still until he was rewarded by seeing a huge panther come up, which he shot. It had evidently thought him dead, and buried him in leaves to be eaten on some future occasion. Michael Fetzer, born 1834, an old hunter residing near Yarnell, Centre County, recounts that when he was a boy a panther once came to the kitchen window of the Reese homestead and looked in at the family assembled around the supper table. He was soon chased away by the dogs and disappeared in the forest at the foot of Indian Grave Hill. Franklin Shreckengast describes panthers concealed in the forest grinding their teeth and snarling while Tom Askey and he cleaned a deer at a big spring near Snow Shoe. He said that it was a disconcerting sound, to say the least. This occured during the Civil War early one evening. The last panther in the Snow Shoe region of Centre county—the great abode of these beasts in early days—was killed on Rock Run in 1886, by Charles Stewart, of Kylertown, Clearfield county, who collected a bounty on its scalp at Bellefonte.

XII. TENTATIVE LIST OF PANTHERS KILLED IN PENNSYLVANIA SINCE 1860.

County.	Date.	Hunter.
Northumberland..	....	1860 John D. DeShay.
x Clinton............	....	1860 Philip Shreckengast.
Somerset.........	....	1860
Clinton...........	(1 Cub)......	1860
Northumberland..	....	1861
Bradford.........	....	1860 Post Wilcox.
a Centre............	....	1861 Tom Askey.
Warren..........	....	1860 Jesse Logan.
Snyder...........	March,	1864 Jake Sampsel.
Snyder...........	....	1862 Faires Boyer.
Snyder...........	....	1862 Faires Boyer.
Warren..........	December,	1863 Sylvester C. Williams.
Clinton...........	December,	1863 John English.
Clinton...........	December,	1863 John English.
Elk...............	....	1863 George Smith.
x Wayne...........	....	1867 Thomas Anson.
Centre..........	December 24,	1868 Lewis Dorman.
Centre..........	....	1875 William Perry.
Snyder...........	....	1869 Dan Treaster.
Mifflin...........	February 27,	1872 John Swartzell.
Lycoming........	January,	1865 George Shover.
Clearfield........	....	1870 Seth Iredell Nelson.
Clearfield........	....	1871 Seth Iredell Nelson.
Clearfield........	....	1872 Seth Iredell Nelson.
Jefferson........	....	1872 Andy Jackson Long.
Clearfield........	....	1873 Seth Iredell Nelson.
Blair.............	....	1873 Solomon Boos.
Centre..........	December 30,	1871 George G. Hastings.
Centre..........	December 31,	1871 George G. Hastings.
Snyder...........	November 21,	1873 Faires Boyer.
Berks............	August 4,	1874 Thomas Anson.
x McKean..........	January 1,	1860 J. Eastman.
x Susquehanna.....	December 15,	1874 Sam Odin.
x Cambria.........	....	1875 Jacob Kauffman.
Susquehanna.....	....	1867 Sam Odin.

"BILL" LONG,
Born in Berks County, 1790, Died in Clearfield County, 1880.
"The King Hunter" of the Pennsylvania Big Game Fields.

XIII. ODE TO A STUFFED PANTHER.

(These lines were written upon seeing the effigy
of the Dorman panther in the Natural History
Museum of Albright College, Myerstown, Lebanon
County, on November 6, 1912.)

At twilight when the shadows flit,
Within the ancient museum I sit,
Gazing through the dust-encrusted glass.
(While hosts of savage memories pass)
At your effigy, ludicrously stuffed.
The fulvous color faded, the paws all puffed,
And bullet-holes in jowl and side
Tell where your life blood ebbed like some red tide;
A streak of light—the last of day—
Gleams through a window on your muzzle gray,
And lights your glassy eyes with garnet fire.
You almost stir those orbs in fretful ire
Which gape into the sunset's dying flame
Towards the wild mountains whence you came;
Revives old images which dormant lie—
Outside the wind is raising to a sigh
Like oft you voiced in the primeval wood.
In your life's pilgrimage, I'd trace it if I could
In white pine forests, tops trembling in the breeze
Like restless sable-colored seas,
Beneath, in rhododendron thickets high,
You crouched until your prey came by.
Grouse, or sickly fawn, or, even fisher-fox
You rent, and then slunk back into the rocks,
And on cold wintry nights, lit by the cloud-swept moon
Your wailing to the music of the spheres atune,

Rose to a roar which echoed over all,
Beside which wolves' lamenting to a treble fall;
And through the snows your mate so slim draws nigh
Noiselessly, with strange love-light in her eye
You lick her coat, and stroke her with your tail,
Whispering a love-song weirdsome as the gale,
You leave her with a last long fond caress
Adown the glen you go in stealthiness,
 . . . A loud report! another! how you leap;
With a resounding thud into the snow you fall asleep.
Your blood-stained hide the hunter bears away,
The virile emblem of an ampler day.
The golden eagle picks your carcass dry,
Wild morning glories trellice on your ribs awry.
Your meaning is a deep one—while your kind live men
    shall rule.
There will be less of weakling, runt or fool,
No enervation will our rugged courage sap.
We will not dawdle on plump luxury's lap,
But as your race declines, so dwindles man.
The painted cheek replaces coat of tan,
And marble halls, and beds of cloth of gold
Succeed the log-cabins of the days of old;
When the last panther falls then woe betide,
Nature's retributive cataclysm is at our side,
Our boasted civilization then will be no more,
Fresh forms must come from out the Celestial Store.

LEWIS DORMAN,
The Famous Panther Slayer of Shreiner Mountain, Centre County.

www.ingramcontent.com/pod-product-compliance
Lightning Source LLC
Chambersburg PA
CBHW060201070426
42447CB00033B/2256